# The Boy
# and the Girl Who Loved Peas

A play for the whole family by

JONATHAN GRAHAM

**Dramatic Publishing Company**
Woodstock, Illinois ● Australia ● New Zealand ● South Africa

©MMXIV by
JONATHAN GRAHAM

Printed in the United States of America
*All Rights Reserved*
(THE BOY WHO LOVED MONSTERS
AND THE GIRL WHO LOVED PEAS)

ISBN: 978-1-58342-973-0

## IMPORTANT BILLING AND CREDIT REQUIREMENTS

For Ben and Lizzy

*The Boy Who Loved Monsters and the Girl Who Loved Peas* was developed and presented as a reading at Write Now, a national theatre for young audiences symposium sponsored by Childsplay Theatre and Indiana Repertory Theatre, in March, 2013. The core artistic team for the project was:

Director ..................................................................Julia Flood
Dramaturg ...................................Judy Matetzschk-Campbell
Dramaturgical Intern........................................ Katie'B Jarvis

The cast was:
Mommy..........................................Christiann Cosler Thijum
Daddy.........................................................David Dickenson
Sue................................................................ Michelle Cuneen
Evan ....................................................................Tyler Eglen
Pea..................................................................Katie McFadzen


The play was first produced by Pollyanna Theatre Company (Austin, Texas) October 2013. Artistic Director Judy Matetzschk-Campbell directed the following cast:

Mommy.................................................... Bethany Harbaugh
Daddy....................................................... Robert Burkhalter
Sue................................................................. Gricelda Silva
Evan ............................................................. David Higgins
Pea................................................................ Aaron Alexander

Other artists contributing to the production included:
Company Stage Manager...................................Andrew Perry
Lighting Designer ...............................................Don W. Day
Set Designer...............................................Jeff Cunningham
Costume Designer............................................... Rikki Davis
Sound Designer........................................ Breton Christopherson
Prop Designers.............. Chelsea Hockaday, Michelle Keffer

# The Boy Who Loved Monsters and the Girl Who Loved Peas

## CHARACTERS

EVAN: a boy of 8, Sue's big brother.

SUE: a girl of 4, Evan's little sister.

PEA: a big, green-headed monster, can be a man or woman, young at heart.

MOMMY: Evan and Sue's mother, not particularly old. Also plays MOMMY PEA.

DADDY: Evan and Sue's father, about the same age as Mommy. Also plays DADDY PEA.

## SETTING

A house not far from here, the present.

# The Boy Who Loved Monsters and the Girl Who Loved Peas

*(Lights up. A dining room table. EVAN, MOMMY, DADDY and SUE are finishing dinner.)*

DADDY. Ahhhh. Those peas were delicious.

MOMMY. Thank you, dear.

*(MOMMY and DADDY start to clear the table. SUE is sort of helping but mostly dancing around the table. EVAN is despondent, staring at his plate.)*

EVAN. May I be excused?

MOMMY. Not until you finish your peas.

EVAN. But I hate peas!

DADDY *(crouches down and puts his head on the table close to EVAN)*. But these are good ones, Evan. Really good! Yum-ahm-ahm-ahm-ahm.

*(DADDY and MOMMY take dishes to the kitchen.)*

SUE *(singing to EVAN, to a tune reminiscent of the theme of* Barney *and other children's TV themes).* I love peas.

Peas love me.

We're a happy family.

With a great big pea,

And a spoon for you and me—

EVAN. Would you shut up?

MOMMY *(returning, fiddling with her phone)*. Evan, be nice to your sister.

DADDY *(returning with an iPad, not paying much attention).* And finish your dinner.

EVAN. I'm full.

MOMMY *(looking up from her phone for a second).* C'mon, sweetie, it's just one pea.

*(Through the following, MOMMY and DADDY are focused on their screens.)*

DADDY. Just eat it.

SUE. I ate my peas.

MOMMY. Honey—

DADDY. You can do it.

SUE. I ate 47 peas.

EVAN. You can't even count to 47.

SUE. Yes, I can.

EVAN. I heard you counting your dolls before. You said, "17-18-19-100!"

SUE *(giving him a pouty face).* Nnnnnnnn!

DADDY. Can you both please just—

EVAN. I'm just saying what she said. "17-18-19"—

MOMMY. Evan!

DADDY. Just eat your pea, and then you can have a cookie.

EVAN. I don't want a cookie.

*(Beat.)*

DADDY. Well, I do.

*(DADDY starts to leave. SUE grabs his hand.)*

SUE. Can I have a cookie, Daddy? I ate all my peas.

MOMMY. Just one. *(Hands her a cup.)* And finish your milk.

*(SUE gives a pouty look, and she and DADDY exit.)*

EVAN. Can I have something else?

MOMMY. You can have your pea.

EVAN. I mean after—

MOMMY. Eat your pea, and then we'll see.

EVAN. What if I eat half?

MOMMY. I think you can eat the whole thing.

EVAN. But it's huge.

MOMMY. Don't exaggerate, Evan.

*(DADDY and SUE return with cookies.)*

EVAN. It's bigger than my head.

DADDY. Are you afraid of a little pea?

EVAN. I'm not afraid.

MOMMY. Pretend you're Godzilla.

DADDY. That's right! *(Pretending to be a monster.)* Rawwwwr! I love peas!

MOMMY *(pretending to be a monster)*. Brawaaaah! We are a family of great, big, pea-eating monsters!

SUE *(pretending to be something else entirely)*. And I am a giant pea! Too big for any silly monster to eat.

EVAN. I don't want to play monsters now. And besides, who ever heard of a monster eating peas?

MOMMY. OK, I give up, Evan. Pick it up and pop it in. And get a move on, or we won't have time for stories before bed.

*(MOMMY, DADDY and SUE exit. EVAN grimaces at the pea, and then he speaks as if he hopes he'll be overheard. EVAN picks up his fork and half-heartedly pokes the pea.)*

EVAN. If I was Godzilla, I sure wouldn't eat any peas. Pine trees, maybe. Or pianos. Or the pyramids in Egpyt, but not any stupid peas. *(He squishes the pea softly with one finger.)* I wish I *had* a monster that would eat all my peas, then I wouldn't have to. I wish a monster would come and eat this house.

*(SUE returns, eating a cookie.)*

SUE. Look, Evan, I got a cookie.

EVAN. I wish there was a monster here right now who would eat my little sister!

*(DADDY comes on.)*

DADDY. Come on, Sue. Don't bother your brother. He's finishing his dinner.

SUE. Evan said a monster was going to eat me!

DADDY. Well, then you better get in bed where it's safe. There are no monsters in your bedroom. Remember we checked last night. Ten minutes until bedtime, Evan.

*(DADDY and SUE exit. EVAN gets up and calls after them.)*

EVAN. I wish I had a monster who was my friend. And it would eat my family, and then we could go on an adventure instead of going to bed.

*(An enormous PEA now begins to emerge from EVAN's plate.)*

EVAN *(cont'd)*. How do they expect me to eat that?

*(EVAN pokes it with his fork. PEA rolls slightly to one side. EVAN is perplexed. He pokes the other side. It rolls back. Tentatively, EVAN licks the PEA and makes a terrible face. EVAN starts to take a bite of the PEA then stops. He tries lifting the PEA with his fork but no luck. Gathering himself, he plunges his fork into the PEA.)*

PEA. Ahhhhhhhhhh!

*(The table spins away from EVAN. It comes to a halt at C. Now we see that PEA has a face that expresses agony. EVAN is horrified.)*

PEA *(cont'd)*. What are you trying to do to me?

*(Now we see that PEA is not a pea at all, but the head of some creature.)*

EVAN. I am so, so sorry.

PEA. You're sorry? I've got four stainless steel daggers piercing my skull!

EVAN. I thought you were a pea.

PEA. You must need glasses.

EVAN. You're green, you're round, and you were on my dinner plate.

PEA. Oh, right.

EVAN. If you hold still, maybe I can get that fork out.

PEA. That would be great.

*(PEA stands beside EVAN, but EVAN can't reach.*

*He climbs on a chair, grabs PEA around the neck with one arm and the fork with the other. EVAN can't pull the fork out and winds up hanging off of PEA, legs kicking and dangling.*

*EVAN climbs down.)*

EVAN. Sorry.

PEA. Maybe I should get lower.

*(PEA gets on its hands and knees. EVAN tries bracing one foot against PEA's shoulder.)*

PEA *(cont'd)*. Ow-eee, ow-eee, ow-eee!

EVAN. Shhh, it's OK.

*(EVAN climbs on PEA's back, grabs the fork with both hands and finally, triumphantly, pulls out the fork.)*

EVAN. Yes!

PEA. Mmm. *(Rubbing its head.)* Much better now. Hey, where's your sister?

EVAN. Getting ready for bed. Are you … a monster?

PEA. What else would I be?

EVAN. That's so awesome!

PEA. Yeah. You know what else is awesome? Tablecloths! *(It puts EVAN's plate on a chair and whips the tablecloth off the table with a great monster roar.)* Raaaawr!

*(PEA uses the tablecloth as a cape. A headscarf. A toga. EVAN is a little fascinated and a little horrified. Now, PEA uses the tablecloth as a bullfighter's cape, and EVAN becomes the bull. This is fun.)*

MOMMY *(from offstage)*. Evaaaaaaaaan?

EVAN. That's my mommy.

PEA. Is that bad?

MOMMY *(still offstage)*. Is everything all right in there?

EVAN. Quick, get under the table.

PEA. Oh, OK.

*(PEA hides under the table, except that its head sticks out a little. EVAN tries, with frantic but limited success, to replace the cloth on the table. EVAN stands holding his empty plate out in front of him. MOMMY enters, but she only has eyes for her phone.)*

MOMMY. All done, kiddo?

EVAN. Yeah, see my plate?

MOMMY *(gives the plate a glance, then back to her phone)*. That's awesome, Evan. Peas aren't so bad, right?

*(EVAN tries to nudge PEA's head back under the table with his foot.)*

PEA. Hey!

MOMMY. Hay's for horses, buster. Take your plate to the sink and get washed up for bed.

*(PEA is still sticking out from under the table, so EVAN gives another nudge. PEA, misreading EVAN's signal, comes out from under the table and sits in MOMMY's chair. Fortunately, MOMMY is watching a really funny video on YouTube.)*

MOMMY *(cont'd)*. Get your PJs on in five minutes, and I'll show you this video.

EVAN. Oh, OK.

*(EVAN frantically gestures for PEA to get back under the table. PEA does just as MOMMY starts to sit down in her chair.)*

MOMMY. This cat is *hilarious*! *(Beat.)* What's wrong?

EVAN. Nothing.

*(EVAN takes his plate and dashes for the kitchen. MOMMY is still looking at her phone. EVAN comes back with a broom and dustpan.)*

MOMMY. Go on upstairs now.

EVAN. I think I better sweep the floor under the table.

MOMMY. That's OK. Daddy can do that later.

EVAN. But there's a pea under there. I think Sue dropped it, but I'll clean it up. You're always saying I should be a leader, right?

MOMMY. Oh. I guess I am. Thank you, Evan. That's very mature of you.

*(MOMMY exits, chuckling at her phone. PEA pops out from under the table.)*

PEA. Sorry about that.

EVAN. It's all right. But now we've got to get you out of here.

PEA. I want to stay.

EVAN. You do?

PEA . Yeah. I'll even help you clean up.

DADDY *(from offstage)*. No, just one cookie, honey. Get your jammies on, Suzy-Q.

EVAN. That's my daddy. You better hide again, but this time keep your head under the table, OK?

*(PEA hides under the table. This time its shoes are exposed. EVAN runs off and returns with a broom and dustpan.)*

DADDY. Did I hear that somebody *volunteered* to clean up the dining room?

EVAN. Yeah.

DADDY. That's great, Evan. Thank you. But you better get a move on, because it's almost time for bed.

EVAN. I will.

DADDY. In your pajamas in five minutes, or there will be no monsters in this house tomorrow.

EVAN. You can't get rid of *all* the monsters.

DADDY. Actually, I can.

EVAN. I bet there's one monster you can't do anything about.

DADDY. What if I turned into the Hulk, and my shirt split open, and I was green? *(Seeing the shoes.)* And would you *please* stop playing with my shoes?

EVAN. I'll put them away!

DADDY. And don't forget all those toys on the stairs. Or no monsters—

EVAN. OK!

DADDY. For a week.

EVAN. A week!?

DADDY. I know—a week without monsters is hard to imagine. Rawwwwr!

*(DADDY exits, pretending to be a monster. PEA comes out.)*

PEA. Sorry about the shoes.

EVAN. That's OK. He thought they were his shoes!

PEA. Yeah, that was pretty good.

EVAN. But you better go now.

PEA. What are you talking about?

EVAN. I have to clean up now.

PEA. I'll help you.

EVAN. But Daddy said no playing with monsters.

PEA. Cleaning's not playing.

EVAN. It is if I get distracted.

PEA. I'll help you concentrate. First, let's clean off the table. *(Lifts the table over its head and shakes it.)* Brrrrrraaaaaahhhhh!

EVAN. Whoa! Put that down.

*(PEA puts down the table and picks up two chairs.)*

PEA. Now the chairs. *(Shaking them overhead.)* Rrrraaaaah-hhh! *(Hands a chair to EVAN.)* You should try it. It's fun.

EVAN. OK. *(Lifts a chair, not nearly as high as PEA but shakes it with enthusiasm.)* Rrrraaah!

PEA. We'll work on it. Now it's time for sweep hockey.

EVAN. What's sweep hockey?

*(PEA begins sweeping the floor while sliding along as if skating. EVAN watches, holding the dustpan.)*

PEA. The broom's my stick and the dirt's the puck.

EVAN. What do I do with the dustpan?

PEA. You're the goalie!

*(PEA sweeps as if playing hockey. EVAN defends with the dustpan, catching some dirt.)*

EVAN. You can't score in my house!

PEA. Nice save.

*(They play some more sweep hockey.)*

PEA *(cont'd)*. Now for the sponge. *(It takes the sponge and bucket and starts to clean the table.)*

EVAN. Cleaning is a lot more fun with you around. I wish you were here all the time.

PEA. I will be.

EVAN. What do you mean?

PEA. You said you wished you had a monster for a friend.

EVAN. I did?

PEA. Yeah. When you were supposed to be eating your dinner. You said you wished you had a monster who would eat your family and that you could go on an adventure rather than go to bed.

EVAN. Oh, that's right.

PEA. So here I am. Should we finish cleaning before we move on to the other stuff?

EVAN. Yeah, I think we better.

PEA. Whatever you say, boss.

*(PEA cheerfully climbs under the table and continues cleaning, making exuberant monster noises. EVAN watches warily, sweeping the floor. SUE enters in her jammies, but EVAN doesn't see her right away.)*

SUE. Who's that?

EVAN. My monster.

SUE. When did you get a monster?

EVAN. After dinner.

SUE. I had a cookie after dinner.

EVAN. I know.

SUE. You should have had a cookie. They're good.

EVAN. I'm having a monster instead.

*(PEA gets out from under the table and towers over EVAN and SUE.)*

SUE. It's big!

PEA *(giving a monster greeting)*. Baaahwrrrraaaah!

SUE. I don't like it! *(She is getting upset and looks like she might cry.)* Is it going to eat me? *(She looks like she might go tell.)*

EVAN. It's OK. It's not going to eat you.

PEA. I'm not?

EVAN. It's a silly monster really.

SUE. It doesn't look silly.

EVAN. You know what I thought it was at first? A pea!

SUE. A pea?

PEA. My name is Pea!

SUE. I love peas!

PEA. I love people who love peas.

SUE. I love peas. Love eating them I mean.

PEA. I guess maybe I should be scared of you.

    *(SUE giggles in spite of herself but eyes PEA warily.)*

SUE. You're half monster and half pea!

PEA. Exactly!

SUE. So you're not the kind of monster that scares me. And no eating me?

PEA. Evan?

EVAN. No eating my sister.

SUE. Pinkie promise?

PEA. Pinkie promise.

    *(PEA holds out a pinkie. SUE looks PEA up and down warily, then they link pinkies.)*

PEA *(cont'd)*. Attagirl!

SUE. Did you know I ate 47 of you at dinner?

EVAN. She can't even count to 47.

MOMMY *(from offstage)*. Time for bed, kiddos!

EVAN. Mommy's coming. You've got to hide. She doesn't like monsters at bedtime.

SUE. But she likes peas.

EVAN. C'mon, you can hide under my bed.

    *(EVAN and PEA run off.)*

SUE. There are no monsters under *my* bed.

*(MOMMY enters.)*

MOMMY. That's right sweetie, no monsters. Hey, it looks great in here! Where's your brother?

SUE. Up in his room.

MOMMY. Oh, good.

SUE. He has a pea that's bigger than Daddy!

MOMMY. Oh, my goodness.

SUE. He's going to hide it under his bed.

MOMMY. OK., darling. Time for bed.

SUE. Pick me up!

MOMMY. You're getting too big for that.

*(DADDY enters.)*

DADDY. You want a piggyback ride?

MOMMY. You talking to her or me?

SUE. Yay, Daddy!

*(SUE climbs on DADDY's back.)*

SUE *(cont'd)*. What if Daddy was a pea?

MOMMY. Time for bed, now.

SUE. It would be funny if Daddy's head was green.

DADDY. She has a point.

MOMMY. Come on, you two.

*(All exit. Lights shift.*

*The table transforms into EVAN's bed. EVAN and PEA return. EVAN gets in bed and motions for PEA to get under it.)*

EVAN. There should be just enough room for you to get under it.

*(PEA climbs under, then sticks its head out.)*

PEA. Hey, this is just right!

EVAN. Now you have to stay under there—no wandering around the house at night!

PEA. But what if I have to—

EVAN. Down the hall, on the right. Don't forget to flush. And put the seat down!

PEA. What if I want to spy on your parents?

EVAN. Whatever they're doing, it's probably boring.

PEA. Can't I go see?

EVAN. They're probably just sitting around not doing anything.

PEA. Can't I scare them?

EVAN. If you scare them, they'll call 9-1-1, and I'll get in *so much* trouble!

PEA. What if we just take a peek?

EVAN. OK, but you have to stay with me and make sure they don't see you. Because if we get caught, Daddy will probably say, "No monsters for a *month*." And you'll have to go back home!

PEA. OK, boss. No getting caught.

*(Lights shift. Some time has passed. The parents enter. EVAN and PEA spy on them.*

*DADDY flops into a chair. MOMMY stands, staring at her phone.)*

DADDY. What a day!

MOMMY. Yes, it was.

DADDY. Want to talk for a long time about something boring?

MOMMY. Absolutely. But first, I want to stare at my phone for a while.

DADDY. I'm stressed out about work. Better check my email. *(He does.)* Haven't checked in 37 minutes. *(He got one.)* Ah ha!

MOMMY. Anything important?

DADDY. Not really.

MOMMY. Me either.

DADDY. Better reply, though. *(He does.)*

MOMMY. Umhmm. *(Beat.)* You think they're asleep?

DADDY. Probably.

MOMMY. Good.

*(She puts down her phone and pulls a DS out from a hiding place and plays. EVAN is incredulous.)*

MOMMY *(cont'd)*. It's a good thing we put strict limits on Evan's DS time. It's totally addicting!

DADDY. I know it.

*(He goes to the kitchen. PEA picks up MOMMY's phone and fiddles with it. It chimes as if she received a message. She looks where she left it, but it's gone. She calls to DADDY.)*

MOMMY. Honey, have you seen my phone?

*(EVAN gestures for PEA to put the phone back.)*

DADDY. No.

*(PEA puts the phone in DADDY's chair.)*

MOMMY. Can you look around just in case?

DADDY. Sure.

*(DADDY returns with a plate, stacked high with cookies, and sits on the phone. It chimes and chirps. DADDY hands the phone to MOMMY.)*

DADDY *(cont'd)*. Found it.

MOMMY. Now how did it get over there?

DADDY. Couldn't tell you.

*(MOMMY studies her phone for a moment, perplexed. She puts it and the DS away.)*

MOMMY. So what do you want to do tomorrow?

DADDY. In the morning, I'm going to look through a bunch of papers in my briefcase and act sort of grumpy. Then, just when Evan and Sue start watching Saturday morning cartoons, I'll tell them it's time to get dressed and go to the grocery store.

*(PEA takes a cookie and eats it. EVAN gives him a warning look.)*

MOMMY. Cool. That reminds me, at some point this weekend, I need to try on shoes for, like, two hours, and then yell at Evan for crawling under a rack of clothes.

DADDY. And after Sue's soccer game, we should make sure we have a long conversation with Mr. and Mrs. Watson.

MOMMY. Are they the ones with the little girl whose nose is always running and the boy who broke Evan's brand new *Harry Potter* DS game?

DADDY. Exactly. We should have them over again some time.

MOMMY. Absolutely.

*(PEA steals two more cookies and gives one to EVAN. DADDY notices that the stack of cookies is shorter and is suspicious but doesn't notice PEA and EVAN.)*

DADDY. So do you want to watch a stupid movie for grown-ups?

MOMMY. Yeah! What do think? A documentary about a dead person or something with lots of kissing?

DADDY. Whatever you feel like … or maybe just the news. That's always depressing.

*(PEA steals two more cookies. There's only one left. DADDY is perplexed.)*

DADDY *(cont'd)*. Did you want a cookie?

MOMMY. No thanks, I'm full.

DADDY. Oh.

MOMMY. Speaking of cookies, remind me to make some homemade ones that look and smell really, really good, but when you bite into one, you find out it's full of dried cherries and gross-tasting nuts.

DADDY. OK.

*(PEA steals the last cookie and exits with EVAN. DADDY looks at the plate, then at MOMMY, then all around. Lights to black.*

*Lights up. The next morning in EVAN's room. EVAN sleeps on his bed. PEA sleeps underneath, with its head and feet sticking out from either side. Presently, SUE comes in wearing pajamas, sucking on a pea purée. She watches them sleep for a moment, and then she climbs up on the bed with EVAN.)*

SUE *(in a stage whisper)*. Evan! It's morning time.

*(EVAN sits up, drowsy, and rubs his eyes.)*

SUE *(cont'd)*. Did it scare you in the night?

EVAN. What are you talking about?

SUE. Pea!

EVAN. No, I told Pea to stay under my bed.

SUE. Does Pea do what you say?

EVAN. Sure. Pea's my monster, isn't it?

SUE. Is it staying here forever?

EVAN. No way. Mommy and Daddy wouldn't let it.

SUE. They don't have to know.

EVAN. They'd figure it out.

SUE. It could stay in your room with the door closed.

EVAN. They'd figure it out. They'd come in here without asking. When you go off to a playdate, that's the first thing they do.

SUE. What if we hid it? We could find somewhere to hide it.

EVAN. Why are you so worried about it? I thought you didn't like monsters.

SUE. It's not a monster, Evan, it's Pea!

*(She jumps down sucking loudly on the pea purée to wake PEA. PEA wakes up.)*

PEA. Hey! Whoooaaa. Good morning to you, too. I thought you promised not to eat me?

*(SUE giggles.)*

PEA *(cont'd)*. You like peas for breakfast?

*(PEA tickles SUE.)*

PEA *(cont'd)*. You're ruining my appetite with that stuff, though.

DADDY *(calling from offstage)*. It's 6:30 on Saturday morning. You kids need to go downstairs and play.

SUE. OK. C'mon, Pea.

DADDY *(again from offstage)*. And Evan, you guys need to play quietly. Set a good example.

EVAN. I wasn't making any noise.

DADDY. OK. Just go play.

*(Lights shift. They are in the playroom.*

*There is a big toy chest here that holds all sorts of things that will serve as props for what follows.*

*PEA gets on all fours. SUE jumps on PEA's back.)*

EVAN. I want to ride!

PEA. There's room for two.

*(EVAN climbs on behind SUE.)*

SUE. Go fast, Pea!

PEA *(moving forward very slowly)*. I'm.

　　Going.

　　As.

　　Fast.

　　As.

　　I.

　　Can.

EVAN. I want to be in front.

SUE. But I'm in front.

EVAN. It's not fair.

*(EVAN pushes SUE, and they both fall off. SUE cries.)*

SUE. Ow-ee. Evan pushed me.

PEA. Evan, each of you can have a turn.

EVAN. I thought you were supposed to be my monster.

SUE. It's a pea!

EVAN *(ignoring his sister, in PEA's face)*. You said you were *my* monster.

PEA. I like to think there's enough of me to share.

EVAN. You said I get to go on an adventure. But then you started playing with my silly little sister. Letting her ride on your back. And you're not even scary!

PEA. Oh, I see.

EVAN. I wanted a monster that could pull out trees by the roots, pick up trains right off the tracks and even scare grown-ups. And you're not that kind of monster.

PEA. You're right, Evan. I guess playtime is over.

*(PEA starts to leave.)*

EVAN. Where are you going?

PEA. Upstairs.

EVAN. You can't go up there … Mommy and Daddy are sleeping.

PEA. I know. I'm going to eat them.

SUE. Pea said eat, Evan!

EVAN *(running to block PEA's way)*. Stop right there.

PEA. Rrrraaaaahhhh!

EVAN. Be quiet!

PEA. But I'm a monster.

EVAN. If you're going to be here, you need to be a quiet monster.

PEA. But I am quiet—for a monster. You should hear what it's like in Monster World. Roaring, thumping, crunching. They have this place where the baby monsters practice knocking down walls … you don't want to go in there.

EVAN. Yes, I do!

PEA. No, you don't. I'd always go into this cave where the grandma and grandpa monsters go to take a nap. I'd go in there and read a book.

SUE. We've got lots of books you can read.

PEA. Well, I do love to read.

EVAN. Man, if I got to go to Monster World, I wouldn't sit around reading some book.

SUE. What if you went to the monster library?

EVAN. I'd want to look around and see all the different kinds of monsters and watch them rip stuff apart!

SUE. I would look around, too, Evan. I'd want to see what kind of clothes the monsters wear. *(To PEA.)* By the way—I love your shoes.

PEA. Thank you.

EVAN. Who the heck cares about monster clothes? I want to see the fangs and claws and—

SUE. I like claws, too.

PEA. Are you two pulling my leg … would you really want to see Monster World?

EVAN & SUE *(looking at one another, in awe)*. Yeaaaaaaaaaah.

PEA *(to SUE)*. You wouldn't get scared?

SUE. No! *(Beat.)* Probably.

PEA *(to EVAN)*. You wouldn't let anybody eat you?

EVAN. I'd run. *(Beat.)* I'm fast.

SUE. Can you really take us there?

PEA. The thing with Monster World is: you can check in any time you want, but you can never leave.

EVAN. Rats.

PEA. But if you want, I can open a portal from this world to that one.

SUE. What's a portal?

PEA. It's a temporary opening in the space-time continuum that allows you to see into another world from the comfort and safety of your own.

EVAN. So … it's like a website?

PEA. It's more like an app, actually. *(Beat.)* Anyway, I need you to get all the toys you can find and put them in a circle, right about here.

*(All grab toys and make the shape of a circle.)*

SUE. I think it's more of an oval.

PEA. Close enough. Now whatever you do, stay out of the oval of toys. Come and take my hands.

*(They do.)*

PEA *(cont'd)*. Now, on the count of three, give me your best monster roar. 1-2-3!

PEA, SUE & EVAN. Raaawwwwrrrr!

*(Lights shift. MOMMY PEA and DADDY PEA appear. They are played by the same actors as MOMMY and DADDY. They look a little like PEA, only more suburban and less hip. They stand inside the oval of toys. PEA, EVAN and SUE watch from outside. Now they all share a mighty monster roar.)*

ALL. Raaawwwwrrrr!

PEA. Evan and Sue, these are my parents.

*(EVAN and SUE cower behind PEA.)*

MOMMY PEA & DADDY PEA. Bwwaaaaaahhhh!

EVAN. Hi.

SUE. I'm ready to go home now.

MOMMY PEA. What are you doing here, Pea?!

DADDY PEA. Yeah, I thought you finally found a place of your own?

PEA. I did. But my new friends wanted a peek into my world. So we're using the portal.

MOMMY PEA. And you came here? I would have thought they'd prefer the Screamatorium or the Bad Dream Factory. They have free samples today.

PEA. I brought them here 'cause I knew they'd be safe.

MOMMY PEA. I guess that's good. Well, have a seat, kids. I'll tell you some long and pointless stories about some relatives of mine that you've never met.

SUE. Pea, can we go home now? It smells funny here.

PEA. Shhh!

DADDY PEA. Hey, kids—later, I was thinking I might rip a city bus into tiny little pieces.

EVAN. That sounds cool.

PEA. Wait, is this the same city bus you've had in the garage for, like, six years?

DADDY PEA. Didn't I just say I was going to do it *later*? Wanna finish my crossword puzzle first.

*(SUE gets PEA's attention and whispers something.)*

PEA. Uh oh. We've got to go.

MOMMY PEA. Why so soon?

PEA. Somebody needs to make the other kind of pee.

EVAN. Why didn't you go before we left?

SUE. I didn't have to then. I have to now!

MOMMY PEA. I guess a short visit is better than none.

DADDY PEA. Good thing you get to go back through the portal. It's league night at the monster bowl. Traffic's a nightmare.

EVAN. Yeah, we probably just need to do a monster roar or something.

PEA. No, it's different on the way back.

*(PEA takes out a phone.)*

EVAN. Seriously?

PEA. When in Rome …

EVAN, SUE & PEA. Bye!

*(PEA does something, lights shift and PEA's parents are gone. SUE runs off to the bathroom.)*

EVAN. That's not fair! I don't think that was very monstery.

PEA. I'm afraid parents everywhere can be a little boring, Evan.

EVAN. But in Monster World? Not to act like a monster? That's crazy! Who ever heard of that? If that's what it's going to be, you may as well just be a pea!

*(PEA plops down and sits placidly. EVAN plops down, dejected. SUE returns, drying her hands on her clothes.)*

SUE. What are you doing?

PEA. Acting like a pea.

*(SUE strokes PEA's head. Nothing happens.)*

EVAN. How about a little more monster, a little less pea?

PEA *(hops up)*. OK. … I guess we should have an adventure.

EVAN. Yeah! And I get to be the king!

SUE. And I'm the princess!

EVAN. A princess? What the—

PEA. What kind of princess?

SUE *(picking up several baby dolls)*. A princess who is the oldest in the family with many little sisters. *(Introduces the dolls to PEA.)* This is Emily, and this is Susanna, and this is Suzy Q, and this is Stella, and this is Beauty.

EVAN. And they are all locked in the dark, dank dungeon!

*(PEA grabs two chairs and puts them on either side of SUE and the dolls, and then it puts a blanket over the chairs: the dungeon.)*

SUE. So the sisters sit down and have tea and cake. *(She begins to act this out.)*

EVAN. Which is all they ever get to do, because they are prisoners forever in the castle of the evil King Evan!

*(EVAN finds a small blanket that he wears like a cloak and a wooden spoon that he holds like a scepter.)*

PEA. What sort of a king is Evan?

EVAN. He rules a vast kingdom and feeds on the brains of princesses and little sisters.

*(EVAN picks up a baby doll and proceeds to suck its brains out.)*

SUE. Stop it, evil king!

*(EVAN and SUE have a tug of war over the doll. PEA takes it away from them.)*

PEA. Poor brainless baby, that's right, you stay right here with Pea. *(To EVAN.)* Why does he suck out their brains?

EVAN. Because they wear too much pink and purple!

PEA. I see. *(He digs through the trunk.)*

SUE. We love pink and purple.

EVAN. And that's why you will rot in the dungeon forever!

*(PEA puts on a silly pink and purple hat and produces a ruler.)*

PEA. I am the knight of pink and purple, come to free the imprisoned baby dolls and the beautiful Princess Sue.

SUE. That's me.

PEA. En garde!

*(EVAN and PEA sword fight with the spoon and ruler. EVAN "stabs" PEA in the tummy.)*

EVAN. I got you!

PEA. Ahhhh! Ohhh! Eeee! The knight is gravely wounded, but he manages to stagger backwards—

EVAN. Into the dank, dark dungeon.

*(PEA crawls under the blanket. Then his head pops out.)*

PEA. It is dank and dark in here.

EVAN. And you have a sword in your belly!

SUE. But then all the baby dolls who still have brains come and kiss you and make you feel all better.

*(SUE has the dolls smooch PEA's tummy.)*

PEA. I do feel much better.

SUE. And they all float up to a cloud and live there forever. The end.

PEA. Now what happens?

EVAN. Long ago when the people of the planets Zorgon and Bathius were angry at each other, all the kids on both planets learned to fly cool spaceships to get ready for war. *(Making shooting sounds.)* Pow-pow-pah-pow!

PEA. But fortunately, they learned to do other things, too.

SUE. Like helping dolls put on their clothes.

EVAN. And how to survive when you're floating through space.

SUE. That's all true, but they also learned preparation, cooperation, resourcefulness and teamwork.

*(EVAN and PEA exchange a confused look.)*

PEA. Now on Zorgon … *(Grabbing a teddy bear from the trunk.)* There was a bear. What was his name?

SUE. Lieutenant Pew.

EVAN. What kind of name is that?

PEA. French, I believe. What was Lieutenant Pew's problem, Evan?

EVAN. He was jealous of his friends who got to fly the big spaceships from planet to planet, when all he got to do was take them through the spaceship wash or change their oil. But one day, he got his chance.

PEA. That's right. One day, Lieutenant Pew's friend, Commander Harley came along. What did he ask Lieutenant Pew to do, Sue?

SUE. To fly one of the ships in a big parade. A parade with marching bands and balloons and horses.

EVAN. You can't have horses in space!

SUE *(makes a pouty face)*. Nnnnnnn!

PEA. Do you know what happens to toys in space?

EVAN. What?

PEA *(picking up several toys)*. They become weightless! *(Joyously throws toys everywhere.)*

EVAN *(joining in, throwing baby dolls)*. And so do baby dolls!

SUE *(joining in, throwing Transformers)*. And so do Transformers!

*(All three gleefully toss toys around the room. MOMMY calls to them.)*

MOMMY *(from offstage)*. Evan? Sue?

SUE. Oh, no!

EVAN. Evil Mommy!

PEA. Should I eat her?

EVAN. No! Let's hide!

*(All three get under the blanket to hide. It's a little small, so various parts of EVAN and SUE stick out the sides. MOM-MY enters.)*

MOMMY. What in the world happened here?

EVAN *(from under the blanket)*. We're just playing.

MOMMY. Well every last one of these toys needs to be picked up when you're done.

PEA. Achoo.

SUE. God bless you ... Evan.

*(MOMMY gets a text and exits, staring at her phone. PEA, EVAN and SUE come out from under the blanket.)*

PEA. That was fun, you guys.

EVAN. That was awesome.

SUE. Let's do another one!

PEA. Sorry, I can't. *(Standing up.)* I have to go eat your mommy and daddy.

EVAN. No!

SUE. Don't do that, silly pea!

PEA. But I'm hungry.

EVAN. I don't think you really want to eat my mommy and daddy.

PEA. Why not?

EVAN. Well, they probably don't even taste good.

SUE. Yeah! They eat gross stuff. Like coffee!

EVAN. And feta cheese!

PEA. I've never been a big fan of feta.

SUE. You don't want to eat Daddy! His chest is all furry, and that hair would get stuck in your teeth.

EVAN. And mommy wears makeup and puts stuff in her hair. *(Beat.)* And sometimes … they fart!

*(EVAN and SUE roar with laughter, but PEA is horrified.)*

PEA. Are you serious?

EVAN & SUE. Yeaaaaaaaaaah!

*(PEA plops down, not sure what to do.)*

PEA. You know, when they sent me here from Monster World, they said, "Pea, we've got a job for you. There's a boy who loves monsters and a girl who loves peas. They need you!" So here I am, but all I know how to do is monstery stuff. If there's no people to eat and nothing to destroy here, what do you need me for? I'm no good to you.

SUE. That's not true. You know how to play!

EVAN. And if you were sent here to be with us, then you should stay and play.

PEA. That sounds fun.

EVAN. But we have to keep you hidden.

PEA. Hidden from whom?

SUE. Mommy and Daddy of course.

PEA. What's the big deal, Evan? Are *they* scared of monsters?

EVAN. I'm pretty sure Mommy is scared of monsters, and that could be very, very bad.

SUE. No, she's not, Evan. When I thought there was a monster in my closet, she said there was nothing to be scared of.

PEA. So they're not scared. That's good. Maybe we could all go to Cracker Barrel together!

EVAN. Definitely not!

SUE. You like Cracker Barrel, too?

PEA. Doesn't everybody? And I'm *starving*!

EVAN. There is no way you're coming with us to a restaurant. Even if Mommy and Daddy let you come, as soon as the restaurant people saw you, they'd call the cops!

PEA. And I guess I'd get in big trouble if I ate a cop.

EVAN. *Huge* trouble.

SUE. You shouldn't eat a cop, Pea.

PEA. But they're so tasty with butter and maple syrup!

SUE. Silly Pea!

EVAN. Oh, no! Mommy and Daddy are coming! Get under the table!

*(PEA hides under the table.)*

EVAN *(cont'd)*. I've got to find the right way to introduce you. Let me do the talking. *(To SUE.)* And act natural!

*(EVAN and SUE sit at the table like little angels.*

*MOMMY and DADDY enter.)*

DADDY. Good morning, kids.

MOMMY. Good morning, my darlings.

EVAN & SUE. Morning, mommy!

*(MOMMY hugs EVAN and SUE, then sits. They clamber on to her lap.)*

DADDY. Anybody up for pancakes?

EVAN & SUE. Meeeeeeeeeeeeeeeeeeeeeeeeeeeeeeeee!

DADDY. Coming right up. *(He exits.)*

SUE. Mommy, what would you do if a monster was under the table?

EVAN. I don't think we want to talk about monsters at the breakfast table.

MOMMY. Oh, it's OK, Evan. If there was a monster under the table, I'd probably scream.

SUE. Would you really?

MOMMY. I don't know. What kind of monster would it be?

SUE. The kind of monster it is!

EVAN. Really nice. And liked to clean.

MOMMY. What would the monster look like?

SUE. It looks like a pea!

MOMMY. A pea! A pea that you eat?

EVAN. Of course.

SUE. Did you think I meant the other kind of pee?

MOMMY. I don't know.

EVAN. Definitely not the other kind of pee. That would be disgusting!

*(DADDY enters with plates and silverware.)*

DADDY. Kids, set the table, please.

EVAN. Sure thing.

*(DADDY leaves. EVAN and SUE set the table.)*

MOMMY. So does the monster's entire body look like a pea?

SUE. Just the head.

MOMMY. That doesn't sound too scary to me.

EVAN. You're right. Not as scary as you'd think.

SUE. Except when it said it was going to—

EVAN. Let me tell her.

SUE. He said he was going to *eat* you and Daddy!

*(DADDY enters carrying a tray with pancakes, sausage, syrup and orange juice.)*

DADDY. I hope everybody's hungry.

SUE. The monster's hungry!

DADDY. I think monsters are always hungry.

*(EVAN and SUE laugh.)*

MOMMY. Don't encourage them.

DADDY. What did I say?

*(DADDY serves everyone a pancake. When no one's looking, SUE hands her pancake under the table to PEA.)*

EVAN. This looks good, Daddy.

SUE. Can I have another pancake, Daddy?

DADDY. Sure. You must be really hungry.

MOMMY. These are delicious.

DADDY. Thank you, madame.

*(PEA finishes the pancake and reaches a hand up on to the table searching for more. SUE pushes it away. PEA does the same thing at EVAN's side of the table. EVAN pushes the hand away. This happens a couple more times. The parents are oblivious, eating.)*

EVAN. Can I have another pancake?

MOMMY. Why don't you finish what you have, honey.

EVAN. OK. *(He starts to eat faster.)*

DADDY. Take it easy, Evan—there's plenty to go around.

MOMMY. Is there more coffee?

DADDY. Sure, I'll get you some.

*(DADDY leaves to get coffee. PEA's hand appears and snags a pancake from DADDY's plate. EVAN and SUE watch in horror. MOMMY doesn't notice. PEA is heard under the table chewing noisily.)*

PEA. Yum-ahm-ahm-ahm-ahm.

MOMMY. Please chew with your mouth closed, Evan.

EVAN. I am!

*(DADDY returns.)*

DADDY. Don't raise your voice, Evan.

*(EVAN makes a gesture as if to say, "What the heck?")*

PEA. Yum-ahm-ahm-ahm-ahm.

*(MOMMY looks puzzled by the sound. DADDY looks at where his pancake used to be, also puzzled. MOMMY and DADDY shrug. DADDY serves more pancakes. While he's doing so, PEA's hand appears and snags another. They eat. As they do, PEA's hand appears a couple more times, taking more pancakes. Now, MOMMY and DADDY notice the pancakes are gone and look suspiciously at their children. Then PEA is heard from once more.)*

PEA *(cont'd)*. Buuuuuurp!

MOMMY. What was that?

SUE. The monster under the table.

MOMMY. Is this the monster we were talking about before?

EVAN. Yeah.

DADDY. What's all this talk about monsters?

PEA. Boy, do I *love* pancakes!

*(MOMMY and DADDY look at each other and then slowly look under the table. Then they jump back from the table, as do EVAN and SUE. PEA stands up holding the table above its head.)*

PEA *(cont'd)*. Hey everybody!

MOMMY & DADDY. Ahhhhhhhhhhhhhhhh!

PEA. And Ahhhellllloooo to you, too!

EVAN. Mommy and Daddy, I'd like you to meet my monster, Pea?

PEA. I'm Pea!

MOMMY. What are you doing here?

PEA. Well, Evan wished for a real monster, because that's what he's wanted most of all.

DADDY *(picks up a chair and stands between PEA and his family. To PEA)*. We can do this the easy way or the hard way. But either way, it's time for you to go. Mommy, call 911.

EVAN & SUE. Noooooooooooooooo!

SUE. We love Pea, Daddy!

EVAN. Can we keep it? Please?

DADDY *(to PEA)*. How did you get in here?

PEA. As I was saying, Evan wished for a monster. And of course, Sue loves peas. So you put the two together and, well—

DADDY. So you're saying they dreamed you up?

PEA. I'm saying that of all the monsters in Monster World, I'm the one for you.

DADDY. No offense, but I really don't think I need a monster.

PEA. You didn't *always* feel that way.

DADDY. What are you talking about?

PEA. Don't tell me you've forgotten about Mr. Sarcophagus?

MOMMY. Who is that?

DADDY. Just a monster I had when I was a kid—

EVAN. You did?

PEA. And your mommy had a castle haunted by the Bee-Gee-Wee-Gees?

SUE. What's a Bee-Gee-Wee-Gee, Mommy?

MOMMY. It was the 70s, sweetie. It's hard to explain. *(To PEA.)* Um … would you mind putting the table down?

PEA. Sure. *(It does.)*

DADDY. Look, if you know about Dr. Sarcophagus, I guess you can't be all bad, but this isn't a great day for company. It was nice to meet you though.

*(DADDY offers his hand to PEA, but instead of shaking hands, PEA picks DADDY up in a big, wiggly hug.)*

PEA. Nice to meet you, too!

*(PEA puts DADDY down and moves to hug MOMMY, but she puts a chair between it and her.)*

MOMMY. Now that you've played with the kids and had breakfast. Boy, I bet they are missing you back in Monster World.

PEA. Not really.

DADDY. I think what my wife is trying to say is, isn't it time for you to be getting back home?

PEA. This is my home.

MOMMY. But that's not possible.

EVAN. Pea was here all night, Mommy.

SUE. It slept under Evan's bed!

DADDY. Is that true?

PEA. Yeah. And no offense, but you might want to run the vacuum under there.

MOMMY. I'm sorry, monster—

SUE. Its name is Pea, Mommy.

MOMMY. Pea, you seem very nice, but we really don't have room for a monster. Do we, dear.

DADDY. Besides, we're gone a lot of the time. My wife and I work and the kids go to school.

MOMMY. You'd get bored around here. It's so quiet during the day.

PEA. Actually, I like quiet.

SUE. Yes, Pea likes to read.

EVAN. And we have Netflix. You could watch Godzilla movies.

DADDY. I don't know if monsters watch a lot of movies.

PEA. That's true, but I was thinking I might take up a hobby. Like knitting.

EVAN. What the heck?

SUE. You're a silly monster.

PEA. I know. I'm not much good for nightmares, or hiding in closets. I don't have long fangs or claws. I only have one head, and it looks like a pea! I mean, you said it yourself, Evan.

EVAN. Yeah, you're not that scary.

PEA. So I figured this was my perfect chance. Maybe my only chance: a boy who loves monsters and a girl who loves peas. Seems like you need me.

DADDY. The point is, we've got work and school and Evan's Lego robotics and Suzy's soccer games.

MOMMY. And Daddy's book club and my Zumba classes.

*(An awkward pause as they wait for PEA to leave.)*

DADDY. So long then.

PEA. Oh, I see. You want me to leave *now*. Well, all you have to do is stop believing that I'm real, and I'll get transported back to Monster World.

DADDY. I see.

*(They wait. Nothing happens.)*

MOMMY. So kids, no more monster now.

*(EVAN and SUE nod a little sadly.)*

DADDY. How about if everybody closes their eyes, and when we open them back up, Pea will be gone.

*(EVAN and SUE hug PEA goodbye, then all but PEA close their eyes. PEA doesn't move. A long moment. They open their eyes again.)*

SUE. But you're still here.

PEA. If you say so.

DADDY. Maybe we need to wish you away … like Evan wished you here in the first place. Evan, why don't you—

EVAN. Pea is like a gift that was sent to us.

SUE. So it would be rude to send it back.

MOMMY . Our house is just so crowded as it is, even without a monster. *(She suddenly has an idea.)* What if we pretended you were something else. Like a corner cupboard. Or a new dishwasher?

DADDY *(to PEA)*. We don't want you to be banished to Monster World forever.

MOMMY. We don't?

DADDY. You seem pretty nice as monsters go. We just hadn't ever thought of having one of our very own.

EVAN. Because it's too much fun.

PEA . But see, that's the thing. It's not about pretending. It's about believing or not.

*(Another long moment. MOMMY, DADDY, EVAN and SUE look at one another.)*

DADDY. I think this calls for a family meeting.

MOMMY. I agree. Why doesn't everyone have a seat at the table?

*(EVAN, MOMMY and DADDY sit in their chairs. SUE leads PEA to her chair. PEA sits. SUE sits on PEA's lap.)*

MOMMY. You all right there, Suzy?

SUE. I'm great. Pea is nice to sit on. And he doesn't want to eat you any more.

EVAN. He would rather eat pancakes.

SUE. After we told him about the—*(She waves her hand in front of her nose.)*

EVAN. Never mind!

DADDY. I don't think I want to know.

MOMMY. What I want to know is—is it safe to have a monster in the house?

PEA. I don't think I'm that much more dangerous than carrying around hot coffee with these two rug rats under foot.

EVAN. Rug rats?

SUE. We're not rug rats!

PEA. Actually, you are a bit of a rug rat … but a very sweet one. Who loves pink and purple and princesses.

EVAN. Seriously?

PEA. And you're one who loves sword fights and space aliens.

MOMMY. Sounds like you really got to know one another.

SUE. And Pea is a monster that likes to play and make up stories.

EVAN. And it hasn't destroyed anything or eaten anyone since it got here!

PEA. It's true. That's why I don't fit in so well in Monster World. I'm not into knocking down skyscrapers or swallowing grandpas in one big gulp. I might get a little rowdy sometimes … *(To MOMMY.)* Just like you spend a little too much time playing with Evan's DS.

MOMMY. You saw me?

EVAN. It sure did.

PEA. And maybe sometimes I feel like eating a whole stack of cookies—

DADDY. That was you?

SUE. Daddy likes cookies, too.

PEA *(to DADDY)*. I won't bother you while your replying to your boss' emails.

DADDY. Wait, how long were you watching us?

SUE. And Pea won't disturb you when you're … doing whatever it is you do with your phone.

*(MOMMY's phone chimes. She has received a text. She turns it off.)*

MOMMY. Sorry.

PEA. I know you have work and school and sports and toys and books and phones and all that stuff … looks like you have a pretty full life.

EVAN *(a lightbulb. To MOMMY and DADDY)*. Yeah … but what do we all share together?

*(MOMMY and DADDY aren't sure how to respond.)*

DADDY. Well … um … now that you mention it.

MOMMY. That's a good point, Evan.

EVAN. When we come home after school, all I want to do is play with Legos.

SUE. And I have to get my dolls ready for bed.

DADDY. And I have all these emails to reply to.

MOMMY. All I feel like doing is watching cat videos on You-Tube.

EVAN. But if Pea was our monster, we could play with it after school. And Pea's good at cleaning up after we play, too.

DADDY. But how do we clean up after Pea?

PEA. There's a special spray. They have it at Costco.

DADDY. Awesome.

MOMMY. What about homework time?

EVAN. Pea could hang out in the attic.

SUE. There's a great big chair up there. And lots of books. And you always say, it's very important to share.

DADDY. Well, now that I have an iPad … you're welcome to my books.

PEA. Thank you!

*(Beat. They all look at MOMMY.)*

MOMMY. There's some yarn up there. I used to knit. Before I got a smartphone.

EVAN. When I wished for a monster, I was wishing for a monster that would be all mine … but I think Pea is for all of us.

SUE. Pea's the best at playing. You wouldn't have to play with us at all.

MOMMY. Oh, sweetie. We never said we didn't want to play.

SUE. Not out loud.

MOMMY. Well … if Pea was sent here … maybe it should stay and play.

*(EVAN has an idea.)*

EVAN. We could *all* play with Pea.

PEA. Yes you could. So what did Dr. Sarcophagus look like, anyway?

DADDY. Um, well, er … I'll show you. *(He runs off.)*

PEA. And what were the Bee-Gee-Wee-Gees?

MOMMY. Give me just a second. *(She hurries off.)*

EVAN. What are they doing?

PEA. I guess we'll find out.

SUE. I don't know what's happening.

PEA. Neither do I, honey.

*(DADDY returns wearing a long coat, a colorful scarf and a stovepipe hat.)*

DADDY. I am Dr. Sarcophagus, and I want to rule the world!

EVAN & SUE. Ahhhhhhhhh!

PEA. Nice to meet you.

*(MOMMY returns wearing a knitted hat and gloves like finger puppets, fuzzy-headed and googly-eyed.)*

MOMMY. And the sweet little Bee-Gee-Wee-Gees can control the minds of all the children they can tickle!

*(The Bee-Gee-Wee-Gees tickle PEA. PEA shakes hands with one of MOMMY's fingers. MOMMY chases EVAN and SUE until they cower behind PEA.)*

EVAN & SUE. Nooooooo!

PEA. But Evan and Sue were very brave, and so they were not afraid of great big Dr. Sarcophagus or the evil Bee-Gee-Wee-Gees.

EVAN *(grabs a toy to help act out the following)*. So Evan and Sue got in a super fast spaceship and headed straight for the lair of Dr. Sarcophagus.

SUE *(has grabbed a doll, or six, to act this out)*. And inside the ship they had the baby doll class from the pink and purple princesses school. And their teacher whose name was Miss Margaret.

DADDY. When the spaceship got there, Dr. Sarcophagus had already taken control of —

EVAN. The planet Zorgon!

MOMMY. And the Bee-Gee-Wee-Gees slipped in through the air filtration system of the spaceship. But the babies were not scared. It was music time!

SUE. Miss Margaret began to play the piano. And the Bee-Gee-Wee-Gees began to sing!

MOMMY *(in the flavor of disco tunes of the 1970s)*. Ah ah ah ah!

Con-trolling Minds,

Con-trolling Minds,

Ah ah ah ah!

SUE *(joining in same tune)*. Gah gah gah gah

Goo-goo gah-gah

Goo-goo gah-gah!

Gah gah gah gah

EVAN. But Dr. Sarcophagus was very angry!

DADDY. Never again can we allow disco to rule the world!

*(DADDY charges MOMMY and SUE.)*

DADDY *(cont'd)*. Rawwwwr!

MOMMY & SUE *(trying to run away)*. Ahhhhhhh!

EVAN. Who do you want to be, Pea?

PEA. I think I'll just be myself.

*(They all enjoy a joyous monster romp. Lights fade.)*

**END OF PLAY**

NOTES

NOTES

NOTES

NOTES

NOTES

NOTES